Paper Feelings

Making Your Way
to a Better Day!

 Kimberlite Kreations

Paper Feelings

Making Your Way to a Better Day!

Books in this series:

The Art of Feeling

Paper Feelings

The Write Feelings

ISBN 978-1-947751-17-0

Copyright © 2018 Kimberlite Kreations

KimberliteKreations.com

Introduction

The Concept

Emotions are tricky things... I'd venture to say that most people struggle with their emotions more than any other issue in their life.

"I just want to be happy."

"Oh, that makes me so mad!"

"If only I wasn't discouraged all the time."

"I can't help feeling this way."

As children, we learn pretty quickly how to either use our emotions as a tool to manipulate others or to suppress them so they are not an inconvenience. Oftentimes, we are as much at the mercy of these feelings as everyone else is. They come and go, defying even description. As we grow older, they begin to compound and build on each other so that we feel many different emotions at once, complicating the matter still further. Slowly, fear creeps in. We are being ruled by something unknown to us, but yet intimate to us, the worst kind of enemy.

However... There is Hope at the bottom of Pandora's Box. People are not meant to be merely victims, stumbling through life at the whim of our feelings. The reason our emotions are so difficult is because we don't know how to deal with them. We hardly even know what they are!

That is why books like this can be one of our greatest tools on this journey called life. I don't say it's a weapon to conquer our emotions, because emotions are not meant to be conquered. They're meant to be felt, and they're powerful because they are important. When a woman births a baby, the contractions are not her enemy. They are her own body trying to bring forth her child. They cannot be more powerful than her, because they are her.

The same way, emotions cannot be more powerful than us, because they are us. We don't have to conquer ourselves, we just want to put everything in its proper place so that we can enjoy life instead of dreading it.

So how do we do that?

Practical Application

First, we identify the unknown so it's not so scary anymore. What is our soul feeling? Sometimes the answer is obvious, sometimes it takes a bit of searching. Certain emotions often act as covers for other emotions, and they're surprisingly consistent. There's a book called "Core Lies" by Sarah Mae that I'd recommend for anyone wanting to delve deeper into that subject. For now though, we'll stay simple.

Our first assessment may be, "I feel mad."

But then we ask ourselves the question, "Why do I feel mad?"

Oftentimes, for me at least, the answer is, "Because I am afraid."

For instance...

I have a young child who is more adventurous than my other children. The other day he ran out in the street and almost got run over by a truck. I shouted at him as I snatched him off that street. He thought I was angry. And at first flush, I did feel angry. But why did I feel angry?

Because I was scared. I was afraid of losing him. I was afraid of the hole in my life that would create.

Why would fear lead to anger like that? Why is that actually a common issue with many people?

Let's think about it. Both fear and anger are similarly powerful emotions. They are so mighty that they affect your physical body. They jump-start your adrenaline, which speeds up your heart rate and supercharges your muscles, making you run faster and make quicker decisions. This can be good if... say... your kid is blundering into the street and about to get run over by a truck. It gives you the strength you need to reach him and save his plucky little life.

But sometimes the feelings don't go away after they've accomplished their purpose. Or sometimes they're misguided. Staying on alert for very long is a huge drain on the adrenal system, and anger often morphs into destructive tendencies if it's not channeled properly. After snatching my kid from the street, I breathed in a deep breath and let it out, then explained to him that I sounded angry because I was frightened, and I reiterated why it's very important to be aware of your surroundings. But even after our talk, I still felt jittery and frustrated. Anger and fear were still pumping through my system, even though they were not necessary anymore. Emotions have a powerful place in our life because they are important. But in order for us to have a peaceful life, we have to keep them in their proper place instead of letting them run the show. One of the main ways we keep them from taking over is by correctly putting them in their place when they get unruly.

If I would have had this book, then I would have sat down and done one of the exercises in it. I would have identified my emotions, then processed them on the paper to help redirect myself from raw emotion into a state of understanding and calmness. That would have probably been easier than going out and kicking sticks in the yard. (Though that method certainly worked.)

I'm excited to be a part of this project. Here's to improving our quality of life!

Blessings on your journey,

Jessiqua Wittman
Birth Doula and Gritty Fiction Author

How to Use This Book

This book can be utilized by a wide range of age groups. The only prerequisite is that the person can follow directions. If a child is not reading yet, then someone would need to read the instructions to the child.

There are two papers per exercise. The first paper is framed with barbed wire - this deals with the negative emotion. The second paper has a more delicate frame on it - this deals with the positive emotion.

When a strong, negative emotion is encountered, turn to a lesson, follow the instructions on that page. It would be easier to rip the page out of the book.

Now turn the page to the positive exercise. Breath three to five deep breaths. Follow the instructions on the second paper. Take your time to work through this page.

As you do the exercises, project your emotions into the papers. Allow the yourself to feel the emotions you are going through. As paper changes into a different exercise, allow those yourself to change over as well.

Feel as the paper must feel - ie. allow yourself to rage inside as the paper is destroyed and then allow yourself to calm as the positive exercise is being carried out.

Feel your muscles tense and then relax. Sometimes things can be ugly. That's okay. That happens. But don't get stuck there. Feel the yuck, but then let's move on to the beauty. There is more health and strength, love and joy, peace and contentment, waiting for you on the other side.

We send blessings and love your way. May these exercises bring you hope and help you along your journey.

100 NEGATIVE Words

Abandoned	Distressed	Ignored	Restless
Afraid	Distrustful	Indecisive	Ridiculed
Alone	Disturbed	Indifferent	Sad
Angry	Dumb	Insecure	Scared
Annoyed	Duped	Invisible	Scatter Brained
Anxious	Edgy	Irritated	Scorned
Apprehensive	Embarrassed	Isolated	Shamed
Ashamed	Emotional	Jumpy	Shocked
Baffled	Exhausted	Let down	Skeptical
Belittled	Exposed	Lonely	Sorry
Betrayed	Fearful	Lost	Stunned
Bewildered	Fooled	Mad	Stupid
Bitter	Forgotten	Manipulated	Tense
Bored	Frustrated	Misled	Terrified
Cautious	Furious	Misunderstood	Tired
Confused	Grieved	Mocked	Tricked
Controlled	Grouchy	Nauseated	Unhappy
Depressed	Grumpy	Nervous	Unimportant
Desperate	Guarded	Overwhelmed	Unliked
Despised	Guilty	Panicky	Unloved
Detested	Hated	Perplexed	Unsteady
Disappointed	Hateful	Preoccupied	Unwanted
Disheartened	Hopeless	Provoked	Upset
Disoriented	Humiliated	Rejected	Weepy
Disregarded	Hurt	Reluctant	Worried

The positive words that are in italics are used in The Art of Feeling, and the words that are underlined are used in The Write Feelings.

100 Positive Words

Able	Creative	Incredible	Recharged
Accepted	Curious	Informed	Refreshed
Affectionate	Delighted	Insightful	Rejuvenated
Amazed	Determined	Inspired	Relaxed
Amazing	Driven	Intelligent	Relieved
Appreciative	Easy-going	Invincible	Safe
Assertive	Elated	Joyful	Satisfied
At ease	Empowered	Kind	Secure
Awesome	Encouraged	Knowledgeable	Self-assured
Beautiful	Energetic	Light	Smart
Brave	Enlightened	Light-hearted	Spunky
Calm	Enthusiastic	Likable	Strong
Carefree	Excited	Lovable	Super
Cheerful	Focused	Loved	Surprised
Colorful	Free	Motivated	Tender
Comforted	Fulfilled	Needed	Thankful
Comfortable	Fun	Optimistic	Thrilled
Competent	Funny	Over-joyed	Trusting
Complete	Glad	Peaceful	Understood
Composed	Gratified	Playful	Useful
Confident	Happy	Pleased	Vibrant
Constructive	Healthy	Positive	Vigorous
Content	Helpful	Protected	Wanted
Cool	Hopeful	Pumped	Warm
Cozy	In Control	Reassured	Wonderful

**Instructions:
Scribble all over this page!**

Need more?

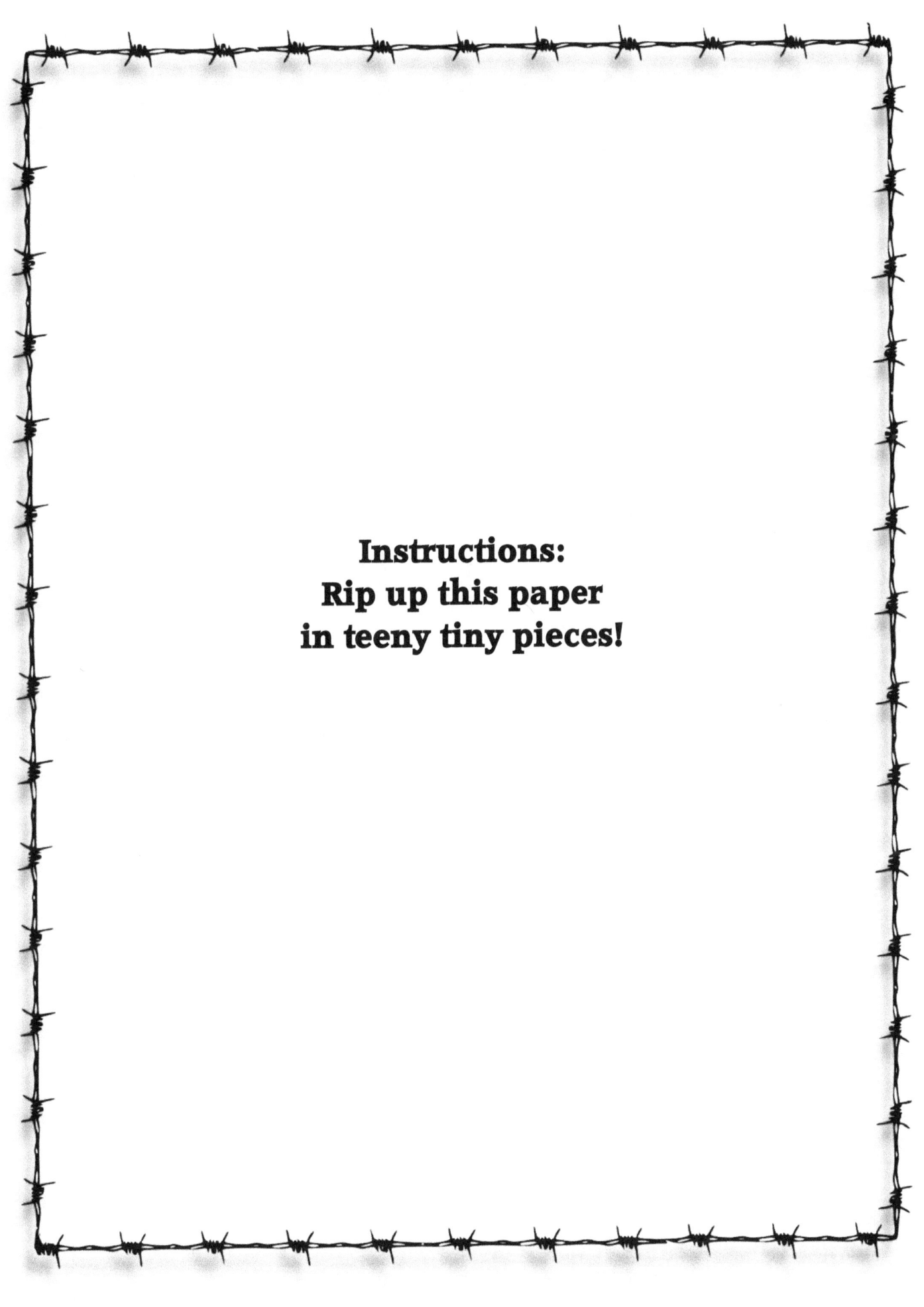

Now.

Make one square at a time.
by connecting the dots.

Need more?

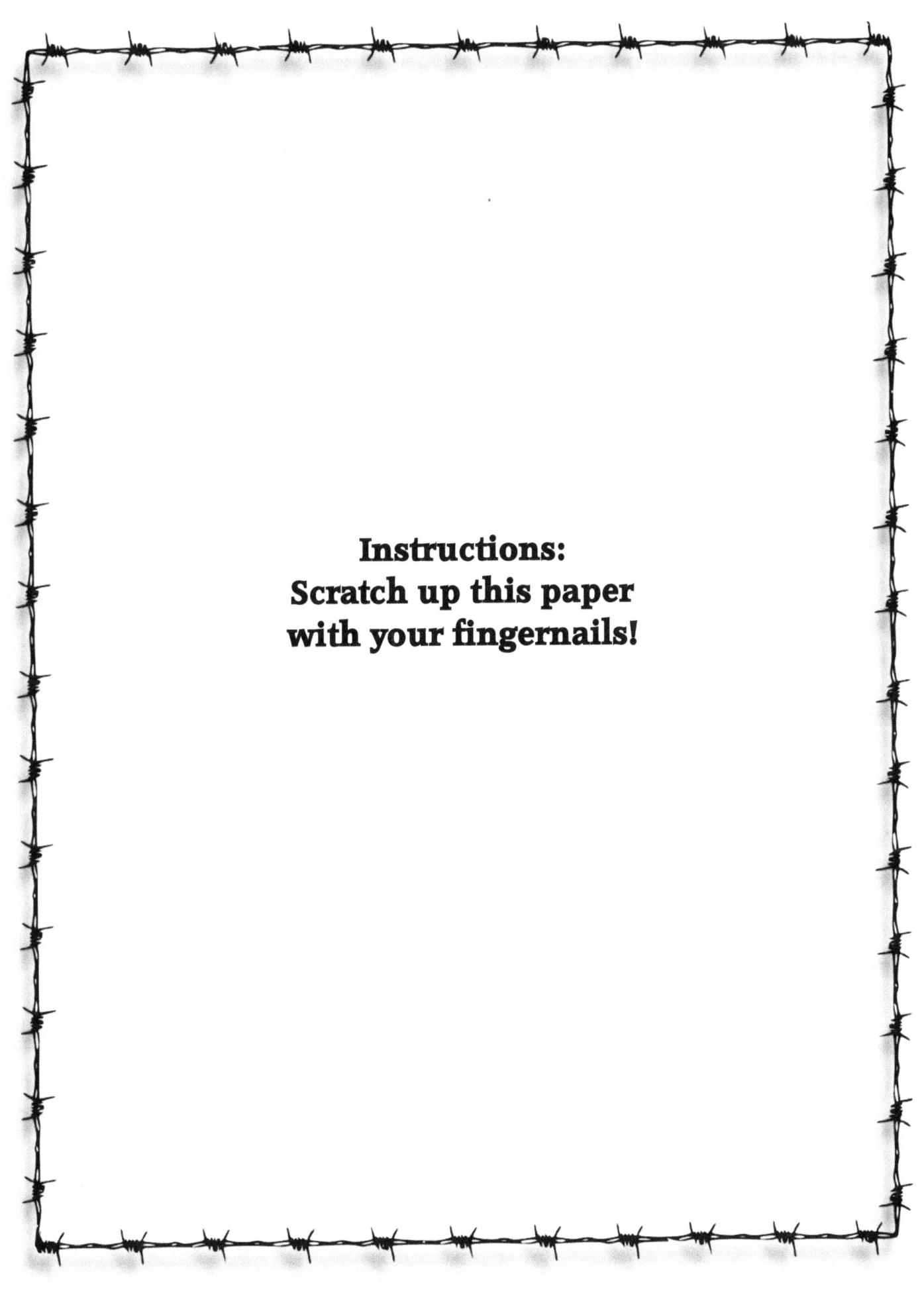

50 49 48 47 46
45 44 43 42 41
40 39 38 37 36
35 34 33 32 31
30 29 28 27 26

Now...
Trace the numbers.

25 24 23 22 21
20 19 18 17 16
15 14 13 12 11
10 9 8 7 6
5 4 3 2 1

50 49 48 47 46
45 44 43 42 41
40 39 38 37 36
35 34 33 32 31

Need more?

30 29 28 27 26
25 24 23 22 21
20 19 18 17 16
15 14 13 12 11
10   9   8   7   6
 5   4   3   2   1

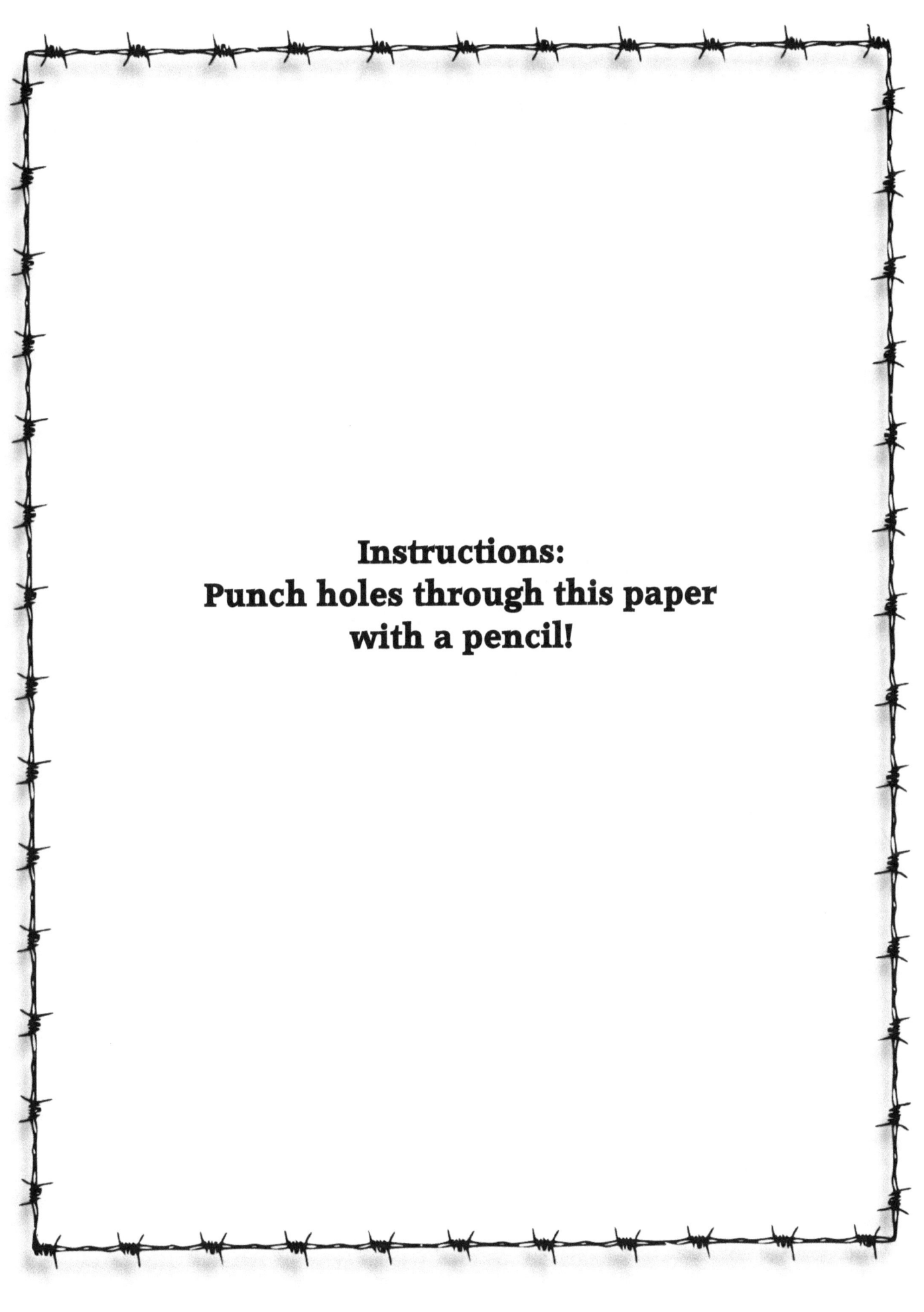

Now...
Draw a line in between each of the lines.

Need more?

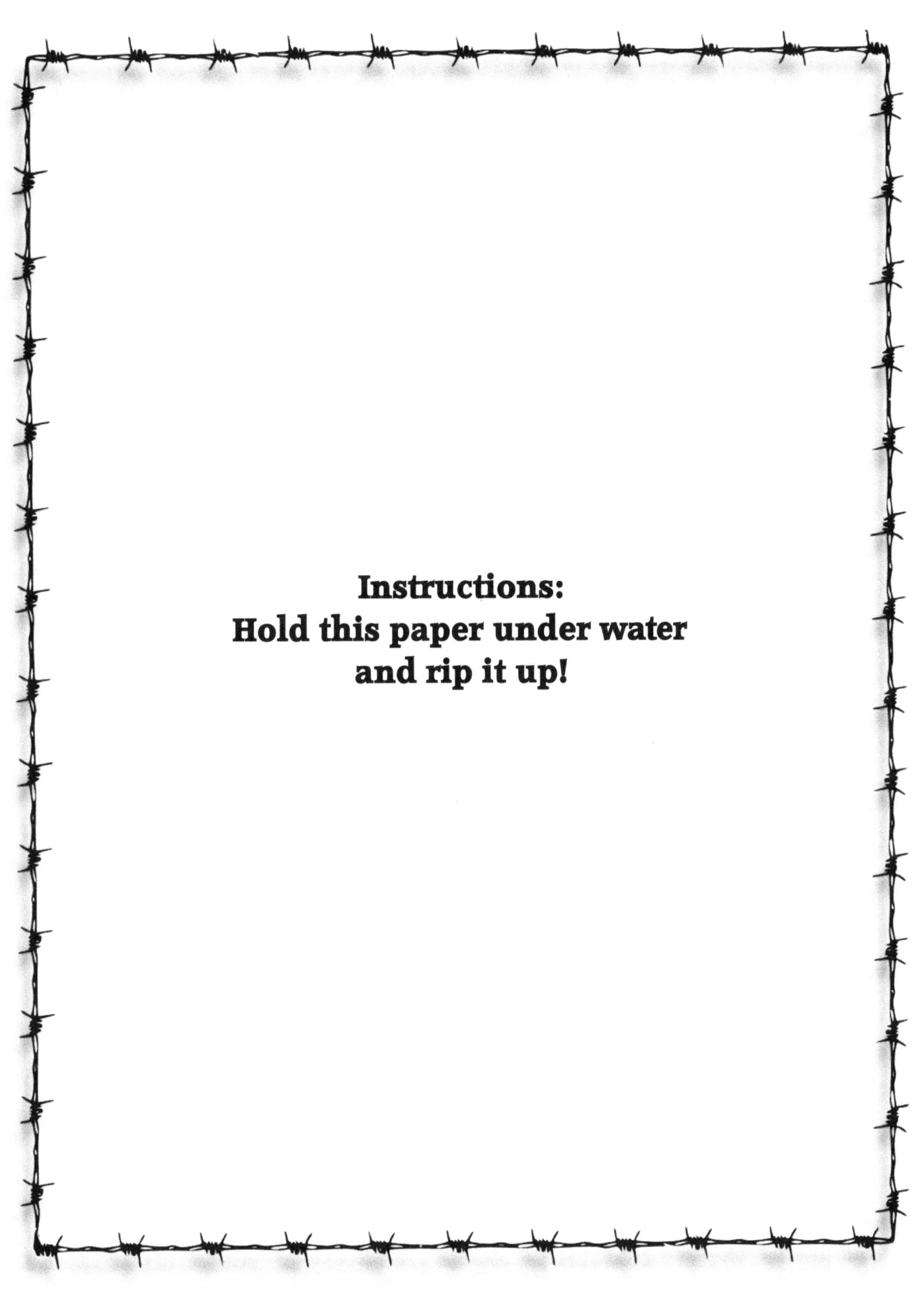

Need more?

**Instructions:
Twist this paper until it rips!**

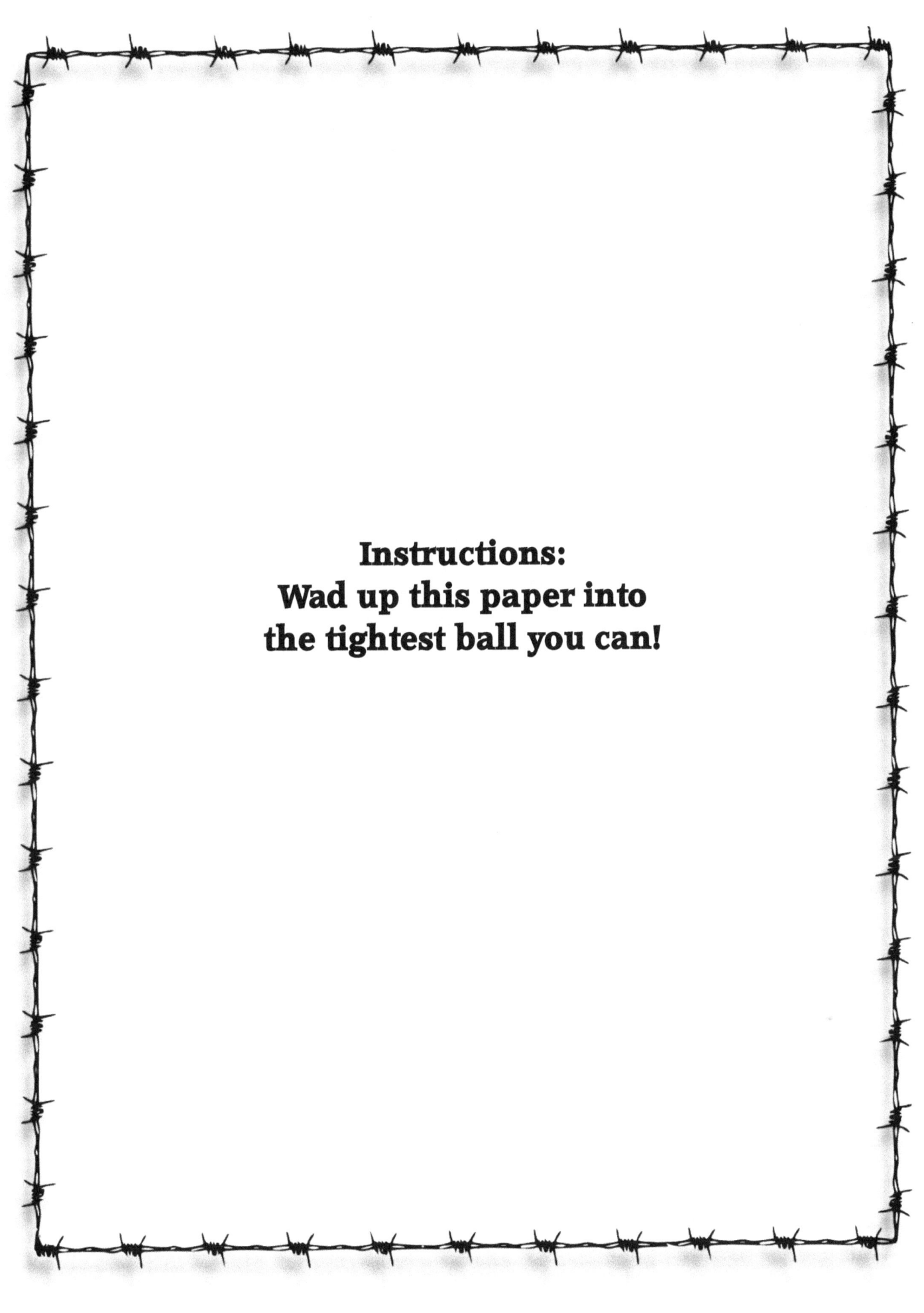

**Instructions:
Wad up this paper into
the tightest ball you can!**

Need more?

Now...

Write the numbers from 30 to 1.

30

Need more?

1

**Instructions:
Stomp on this paper
over and over!**

Now...
Trace the bubbles.

Need more?

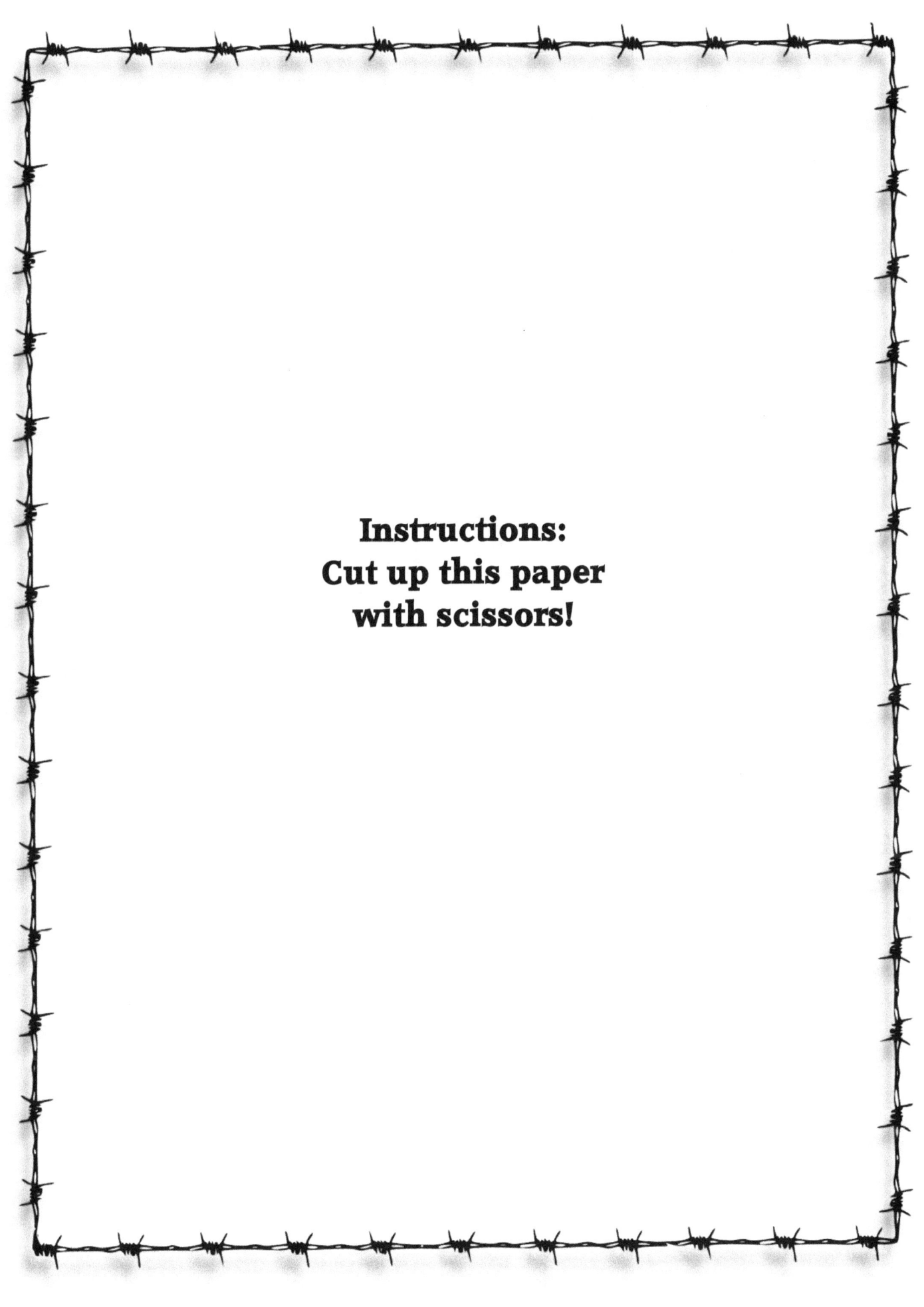

**Instructions:
Cut up this paper
with scissors!**

A B C D
E F G H I
J K L M

Need more?

N O P Q
R S T U V
W X Y Z

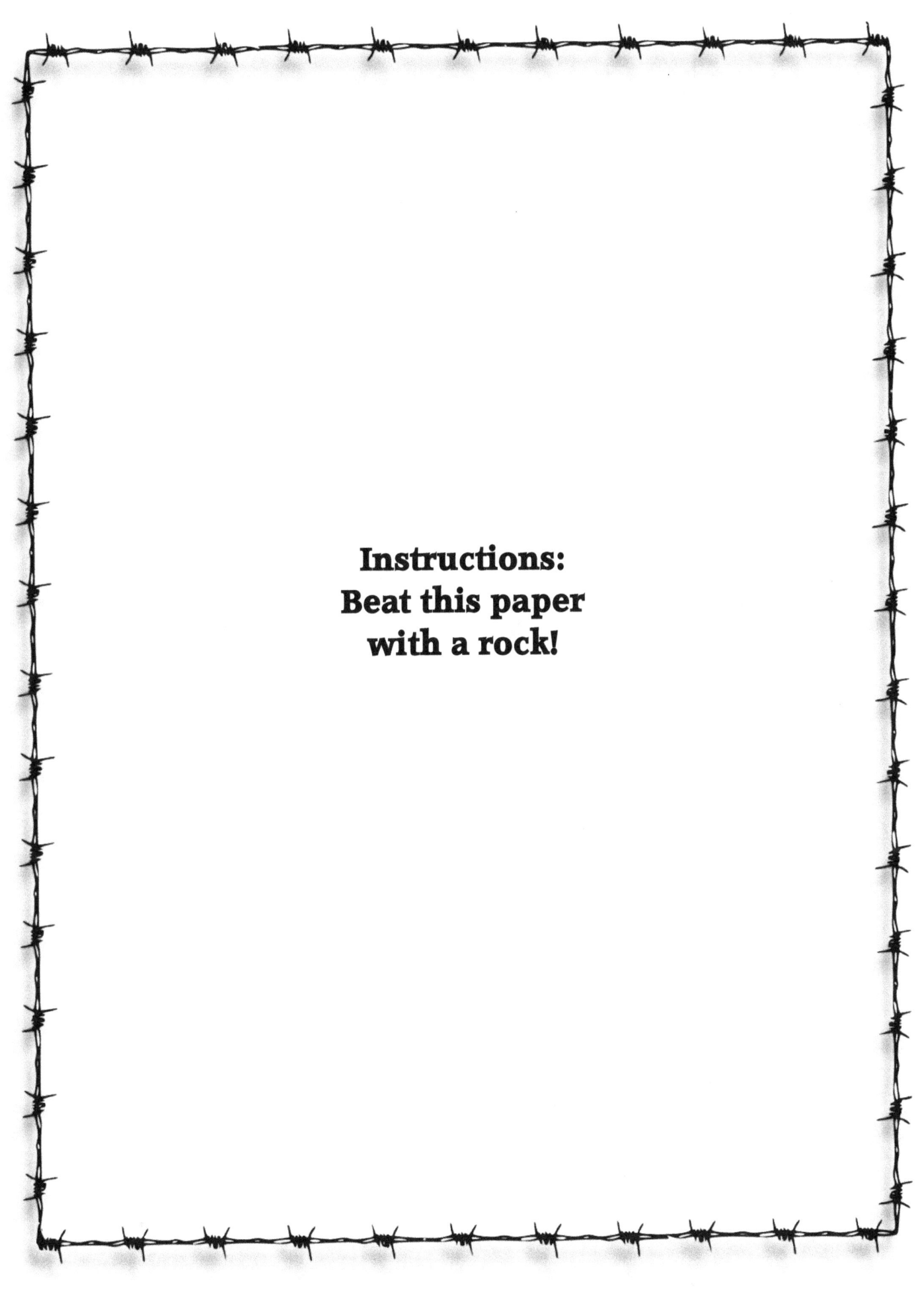

Now...
Color the rain drops.

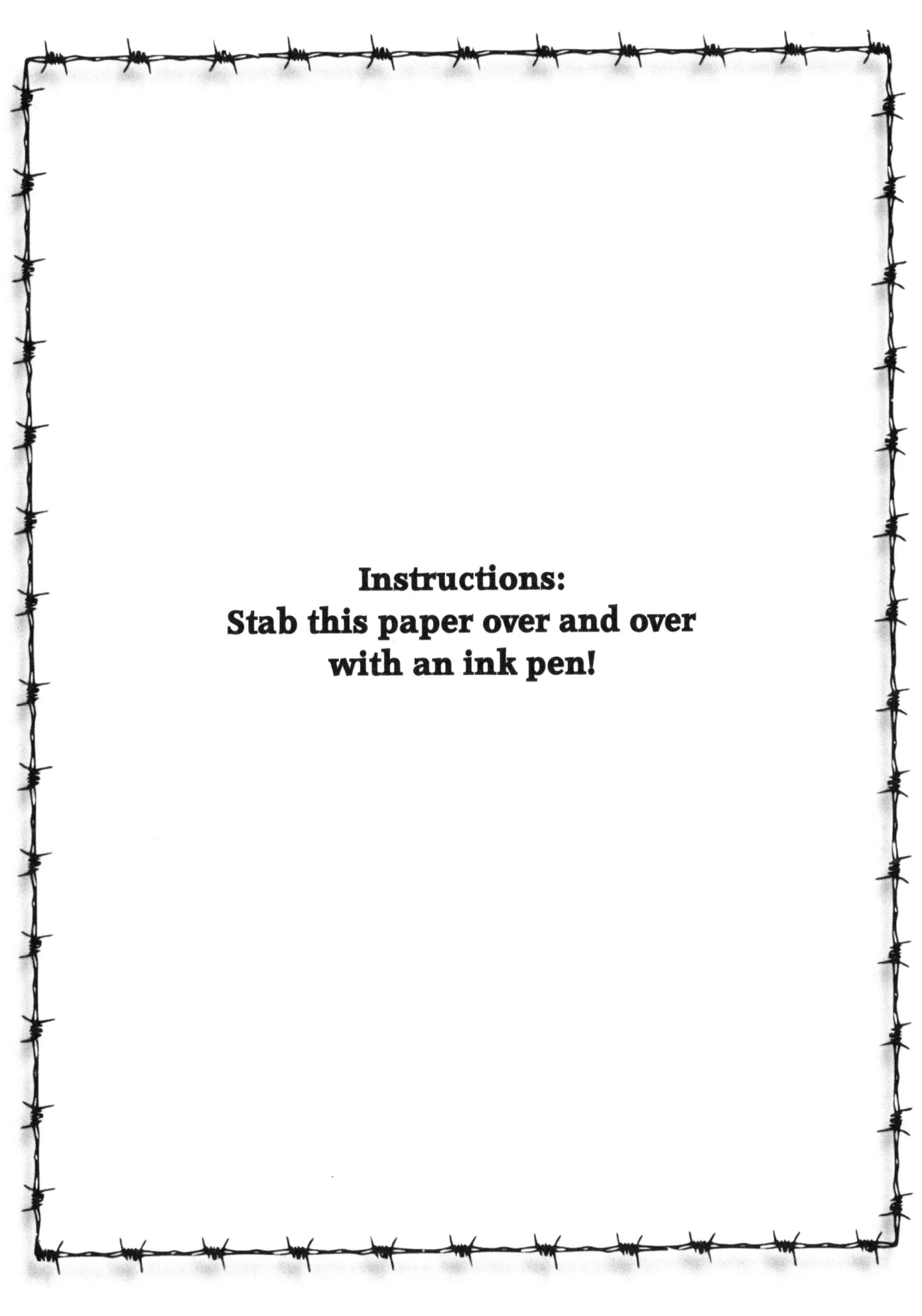

**Instructions:
Stab this paper over and over with an ink pen!**

Now
Draw vertical lines
between the lines.

**Instructions:
Make short pencil marks
all over this paper!**

A B C D
E F G H I
J K L M

Now...
Trace the letters.

N O P Q
R S T U V
W X Y Z

A B C D
E F G H I
J K L M

Need more?

N O P Q
R S T U V
W X Y Z

**Instructions:
Stomp on this paper and
twist your foot until it rips up!**

Now... Color the quilt.

Need more?

Now...
Color the snowflakes.

Now...
Trace the stars.

Need more?

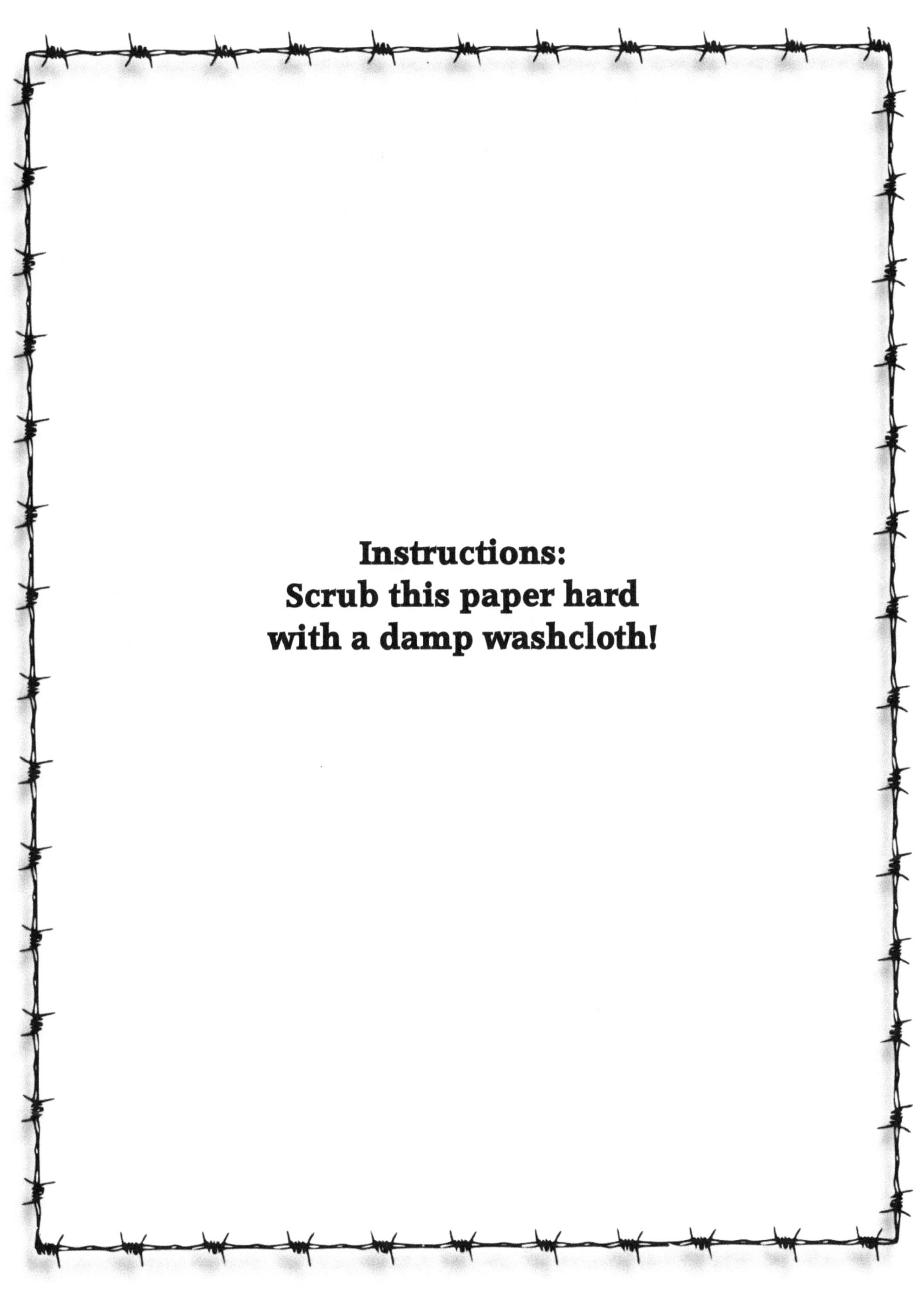

**Instructions:
Scrub this paper hard
with a damp washcloth!**

Now...
Color the honeycomb.

A __ __ __

__ __ __ __

__ __ __ __

Now...
Write the letters.

__ __ __ __

__ __ __ __

__ __ __ Z

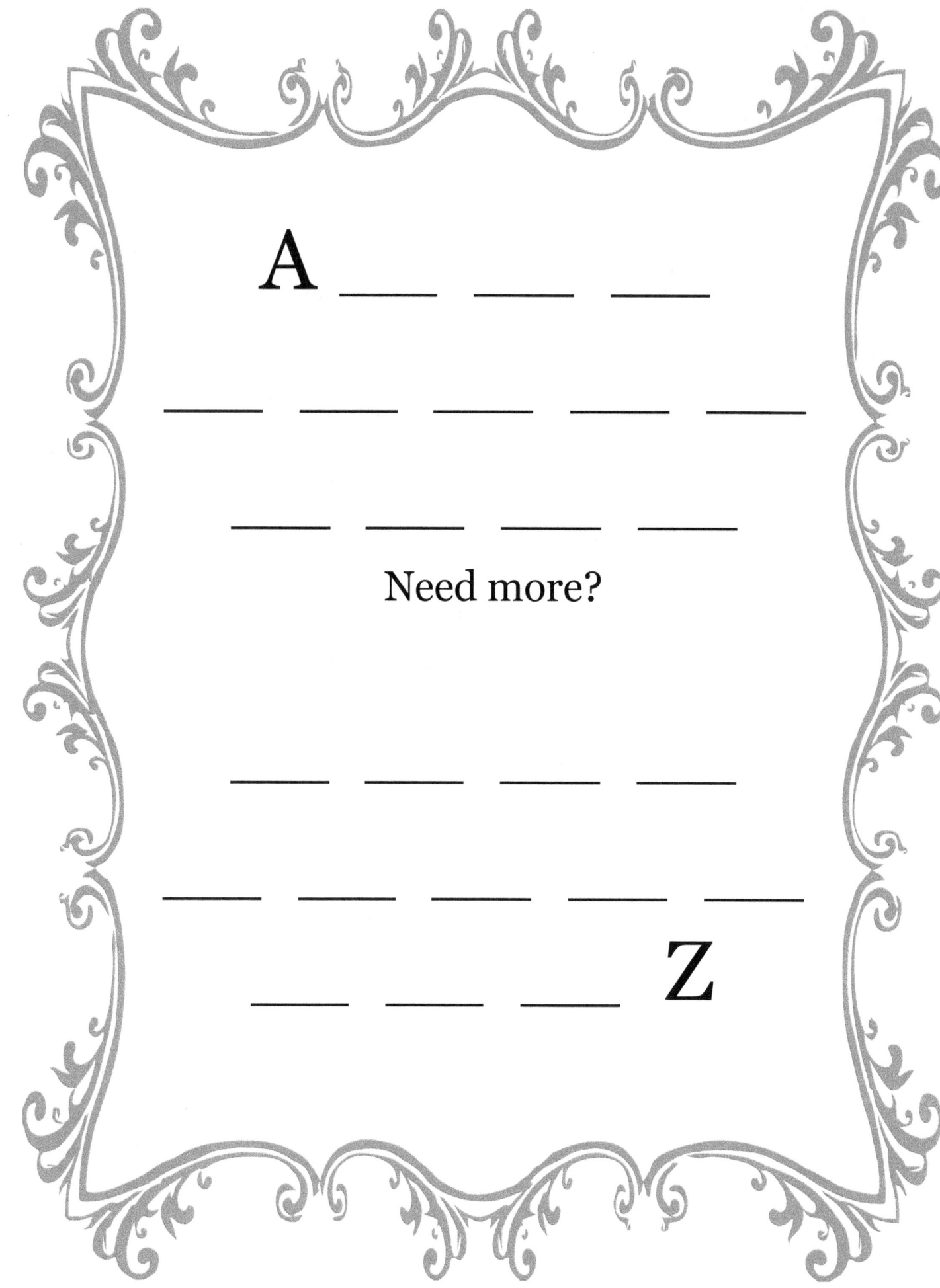

A _ _ _ _

_ _ _ _ _

_ _ _ _ _

Need more?

_ _ _ _ _

_ _ _ _ Z

_ _ _ _

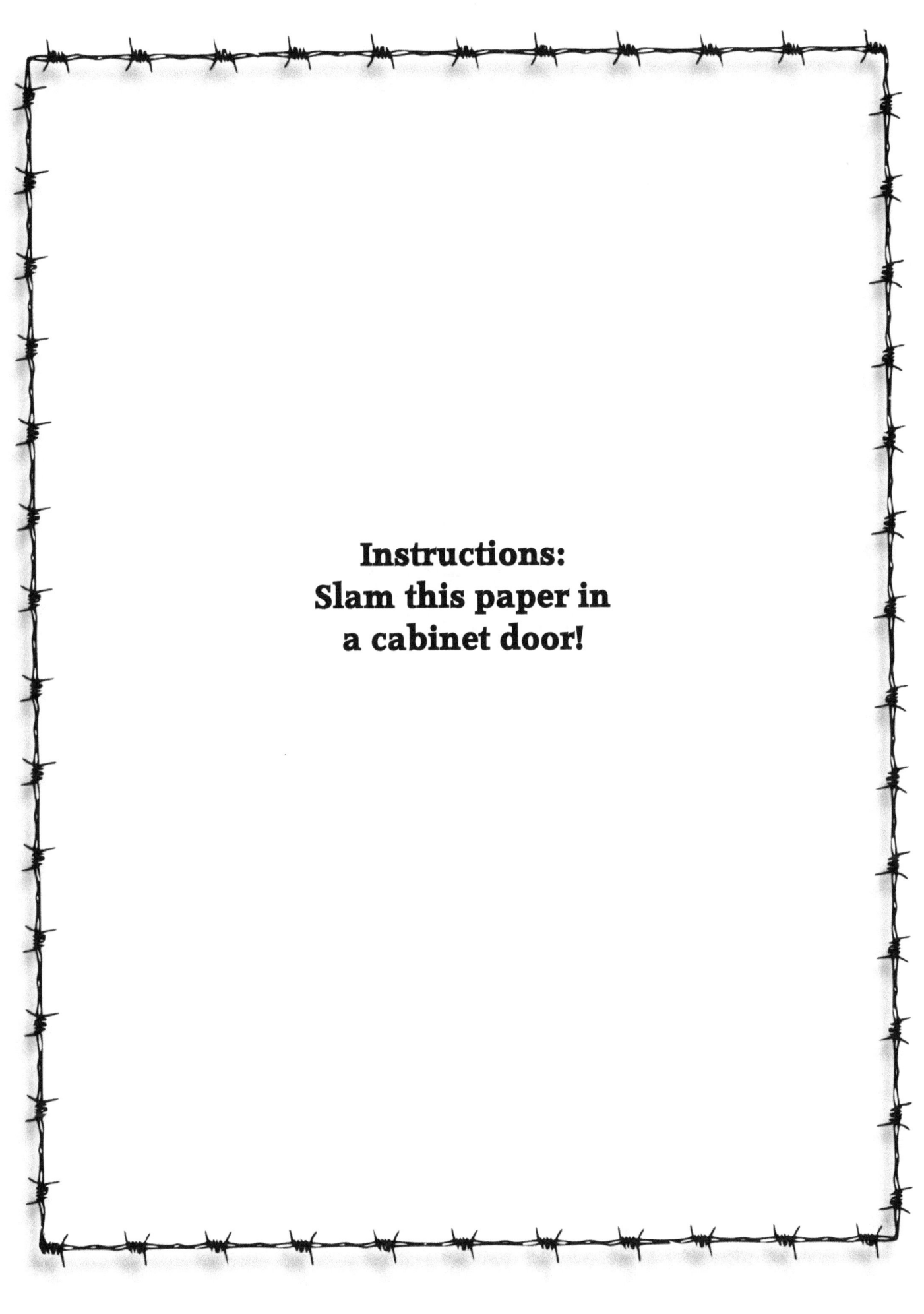

Need more?

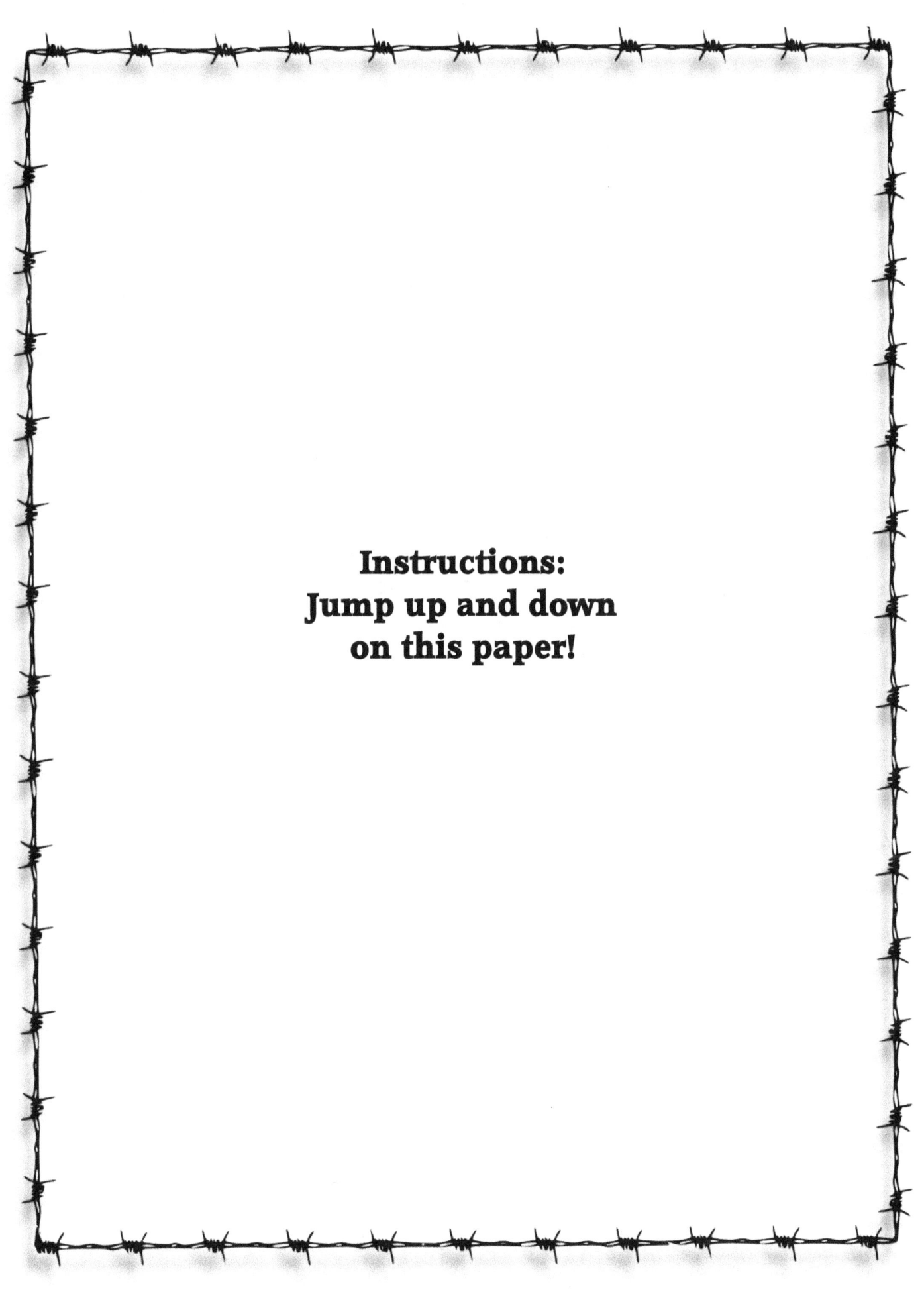

**Instructions:
Jump up and down
on this paper!**

Need more?

Now...
Color every other square.

Need more?

**Instructions:
Wad up this paper and
throw it against the wall!**

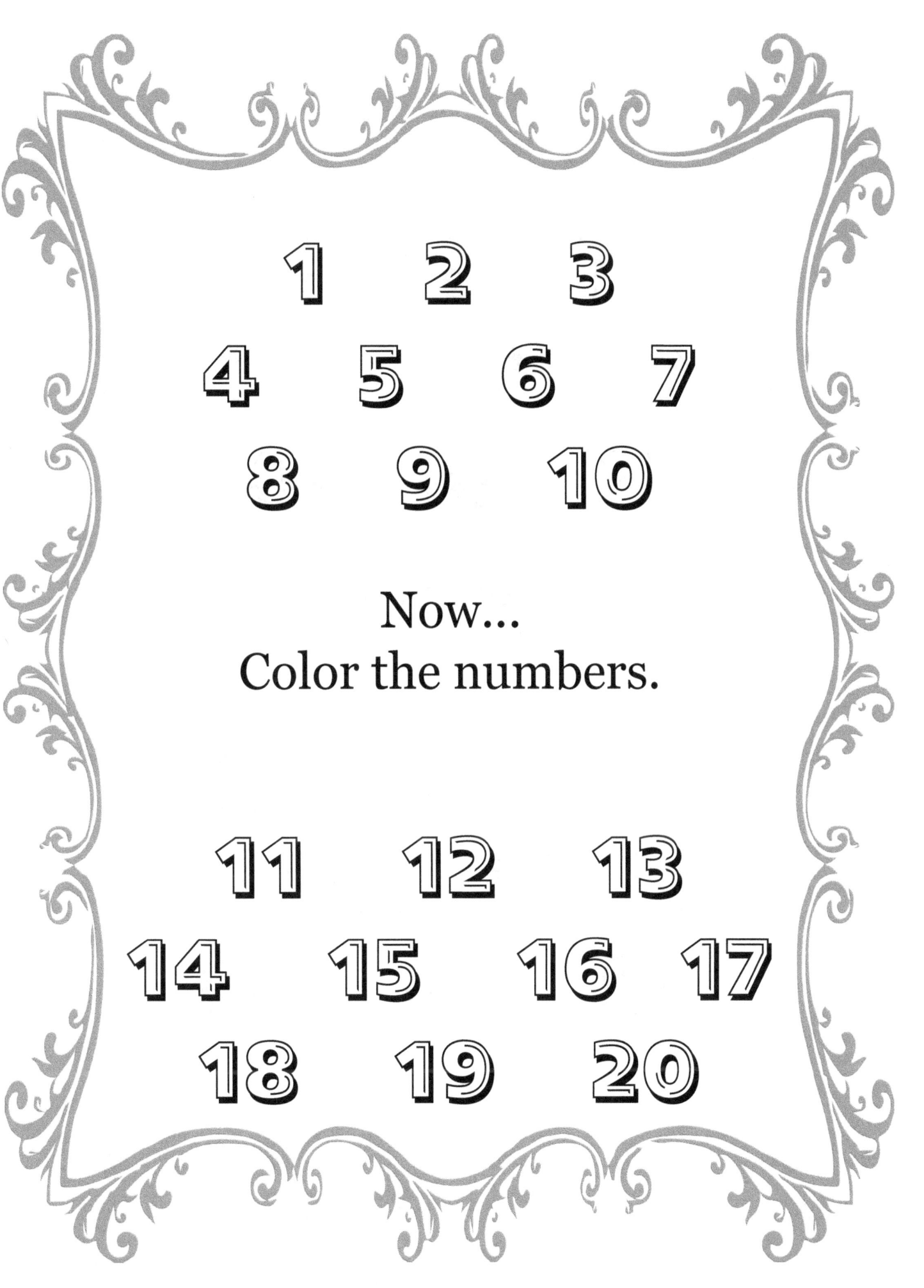

**Instructions:
Chew up this paper
and spit it in the trash!**

Now... Color the triangles.

**Instructions:
Shake this paper violently!**

Now...
Be creative and
do your own thing.

Need more?

Now...
Be creative and
do your own thing.

Now...
Be creative and
do your own thing.

Need more?

Now...
Be creative and
do your own thing.

Need more?

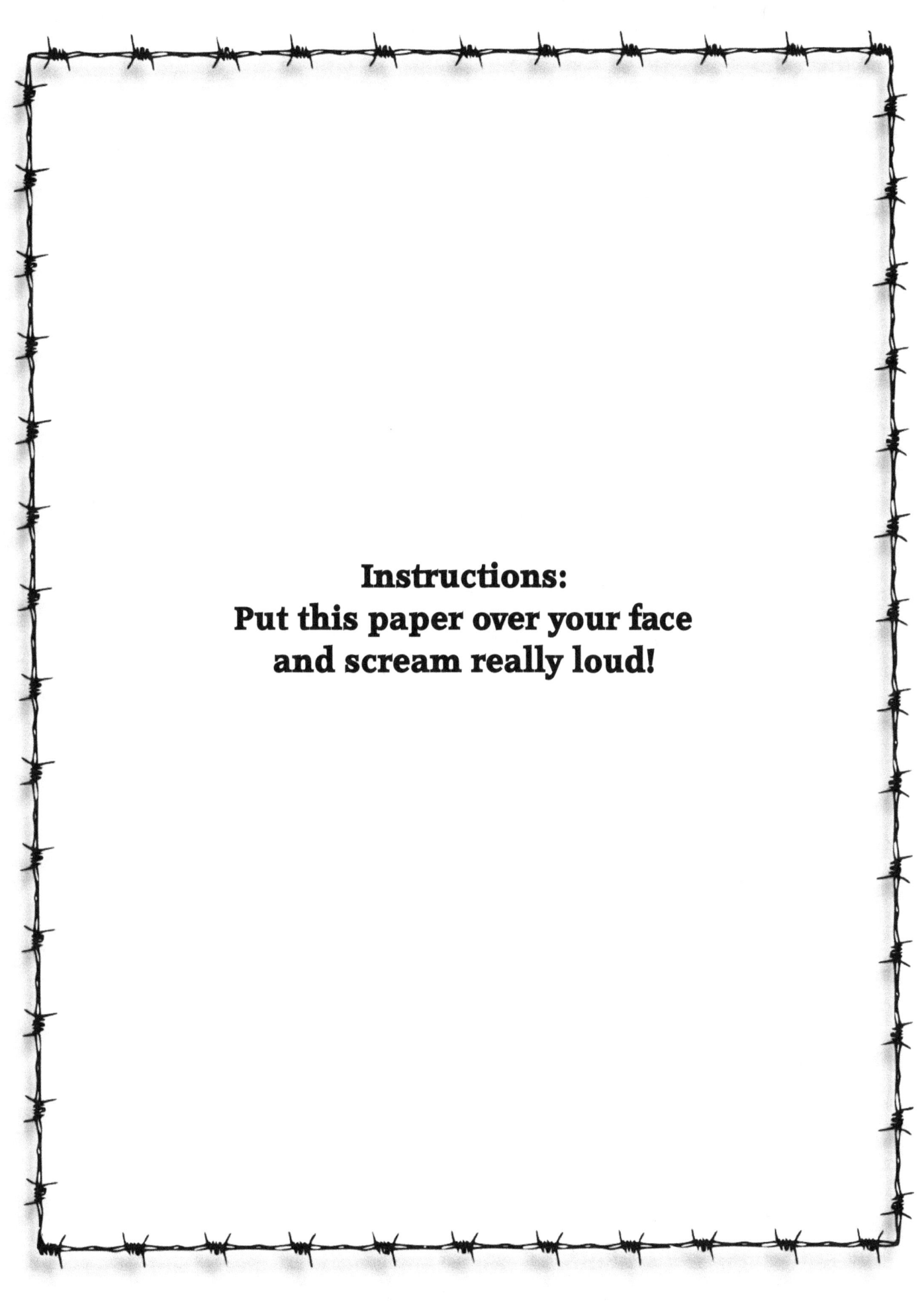

Now...
Be creative and
do your own thing.

Need more?

If you feel this book has been helpful,
please consider writing a review
and letting others know of our materials.

Thanks!

Kimberlite
Kreations

KimberliteKreations.com

www.ingramcontent.com/pod-product-compliance
Lightning Source LLC
Chambersburg PA
CBHW081336080526
44588CB00017B/2637